CONTENTS

Dear Reader

You're about to find out about forces. And if you reply 'So who's forcing what?' then you really need to know that forces are vital in everyday life. Just imagine this next bit...

It's your school sports day and you are in a tug of war competition. That's when two teams are pulling on a rope in opposite directions. The winner is the team that pulls a marker on the rope over a central line.

Oh dear – looks like the other side is winning! What can you do? Clue: Use forces. Second clue: Use an elephant (answer below).

Answer:
Tie the elephant to the end of your rope and persuade it to walk off in the direction your team is pulling!

Forces are constantly in action, shifting everything from snails to space rockets and parrots to planets. So you see, if something moves at all it moves because of forces and that is what this book is all about! It's about a universe full of action and excitement... and forces. You'll uncover fascinating facts such as what happens when a fly splats on a windscreen, and read a chilling story about a ghost on two wheels.

But first you'll need to use some force of your own...

1 Grasp corner of page forcefully between finger and thumb.

2 Use wrist action force to lift corner of page.

3 Now for the big one – lift the full weight of the paper – phew! And turn it over...

UNDERSTANDING FORCES

A universe full of forces sounds like a whole lot of learning – or even a whole lifetime of learning. Fortunately, we've forced this knowledge into bite-sized chunks of information so you don't have to force your brain to remember it all.

WHAT IS A FORCE?

Forces cause or change the movement of an object. A force might push or pull an object, and forces can also make things speed up, change direction and slow down.

pulling force

pushing force

MEASURING FORCE

Scientists measure a force in newtons (N). A newton is a unit of measurement named after scientific superstar Isaac Newton (see page 32).

A spring balance is often used to measure a force. The weight pulls the spring balance down and the force is measured in newtons.

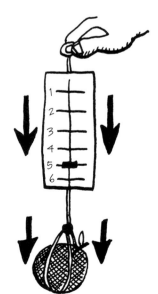
spring balance

GRAVITY

Leap in the air and you will return to Earth with a bump. The force that pulls you is gravity tugging you towards the centre of the Earth! (By the way, the reason you don't sink right to the centre of the Earth is because the ground gets in the way!)

Help - it's gravity!

Swampy ground doesn't stop you sinking!

Gravity is a pulling force between any two objects. The more material an object contains (scientists say the more mass it has) the stronger its gravitational pull. That's why the Earth (which has a bit more mass than you) can pull you down. On Earth, the force of gravity is measured in terms of weight.

MAGNETISM

Magnetism is a force made by magnets – amazing that! When you put a magnet next to certain metals, such as iron or nickel, the magnetic force can pull the metal object towards the magnet and even lift it off the ground. Magnets pick up certain metals because the magnetic force pulls on the tiny atoms that make up the metals.

Magnetic force is made by countless tiny specks of energy inside the magnet, and it is strongest at the magnetic poles. One pole is called the north pole and the other is called the south pole.

If you place two magnets so that their north or south poles are close together, the magnetic force will push the magnets apart.

North pole   South pole

If two magnets are placed with their north and south poles close together the two magnets will attract each other (or pull towards each other).

BELIEVE IT OR NOT!
Scientists have found out that a moving magnetic force can make electricity flow in a wire, and electricity flowing in a wire gives off a magnetic force.

Electricity heats up wire in a light bulb until it glows.

Springs and Stretching

When springs or elastic bands are stretched they create
a stretching force on whatever is stretching them. You can
prove this by stretching an elastic band between your fingers.
Can you feel the band pulling on your fingers? All substances
differ in their elasticity.

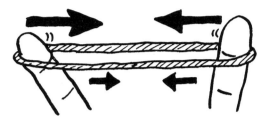

Alternatively, you can squeeze a spring until it's coiled tight
and you can feel the spring pushing back. This force can be
released to power a machine such as a clock or a watch or
even a clockwork mouse. And you will find springs in beds
and sofas and under your bike saddle to support your weight.

Springs under a bike
saddle soak up the force
of bumps in the road
and support this overweight
scientist's huge backside.

Springs push
upwards equally hard.

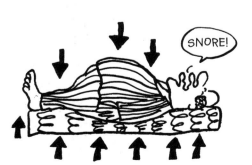

Heavy body squashes springs.
Springs push upwards.

And springs help the scientist
to sleep well at night.

BALANCED FORCES

Forces are balanced when they are equally strong in all directions. This means that the forces cancel each other out so that things do not move. The balancing of forces explains why objects float (see page 14) but they are really useful on dry land too. When you stand or walk the forces around you are balanced – this fact is vital for tightrope walkers!

force of gravity pulls downwards

gravity balanced by the rope pushing upwards

So, the force of gravity pulling down equals the force of the rope pushing upwards.

If you are sitting on a chair reading this book then you are experiencing balanced forces. Your weight pushes down on the chair, but the chair pushes up with an equal force, so the two forces are balanced.

And, of course, the tug of war teams on page 4 made more or less balanced forces too.

Unbalanced Forces

When forces are unbalanced, things start to move.

Here, the force of gravity is greater than the air resistance (see page 15) or upthrust (see page 14). So the cat plummets to the ground. Only eight lives left!

Friction

Even the smoothest surfaces appear rough and uneven when they are seen close up. When surfaces rub together the uneven bits catch and cause the slowing force we call friction.

Here are some uses for friction...

Violinists put sticky rosin on their bows. This causes friction with the strings and results in a rapid jerky movement of the bow that can produce beautiful music (or something like a cat with toothache).

Friction between a match head and a matchbox produces heat that causes the match head to catch fire.

Friction between an object and the air makes heat. So, friction between meteorites and the air causes meteorites to become burning hot before they hit the Earth.

Although friction slows things down, it can be very useful. Friction between your feet and the floor stops you falling over.

friction between your shoe and the floor stops your foot slipping

smooth polished floor, smooth socks

WARNING
So, remember NEVER to try to run in socks on polished floors!

There is more friction between two rough surfaces and less friction between two smooth surfaces.

You can measure friction by attaching an object to a spring balance and dragging it over a surface. The force of friction can be measured in Newtons.

Newton's Laws

Everything in the universe moves according to laws set down by scientific genius Isaac Newton (1642–1727) over 300 years ago. Mind you, Newton didn't make these laws, he simply discovered how forces had been operating since the beginning of time. Here's how Newton's laws affect Mr Jones and his used car...

LAW 1   Objects don't move unless acted upon by a force. When they do move, they travel in a straight line unless another force alters their direction.

The car only moves as a result of the force from its engine. When the engine cuts out, the vehicle carries on moving in a straight line. Eventually, friction slows the car down.

friction between the wheels and the moving parts inside the car

friction between the air and the car

friction between the wheels and the road

LAW 2   Objects move in the same direction as the force.

The Jones family try to push start the car. The car moves in the direction of their push.

LAW 3 Objects push back just as hard against the force that pushes them.

car pushes back on the children

Law three sounds odd, but if you think about it, it makes sense. How can you lean against a wall if the wall doesn't push back and keep you upright.

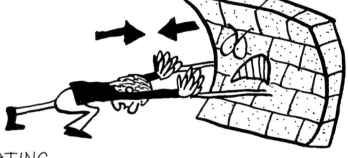

FLOATING

Here's some good news for swimmers. There's a force in water that helps you to float! When you're swimming, the water pushes back with an upward force called upthrust. Here's how it works. When you get in the water your body pushes water out of the way. As long as your body weighs less than the water you push aside, the upthrust from the water will help you float. In fact, you don't float terribly well because your body is mainly made up of water which, of course, weighs the same as the water you are swimming in!

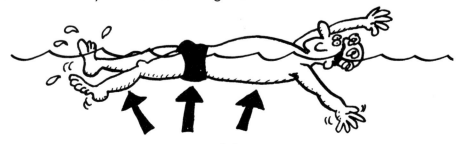

DRAG

When an object moves through air or water, friction with the air or water slows it down. This is called air or water resistance and the force involved is called drag. Smooth streamlined shapes reduce the amount of friction and things can move very fast. Let's compare a bird and a shark.

As the bird flies through the air it's slowed down by drag. At the same time, gravity tries to pull the bird down. So, to remain in the air, the bird flaps its wings to make the air flow over them and lift it up. A bird's wings are shaped so that they cut smoothly through the air and keep down the drag.

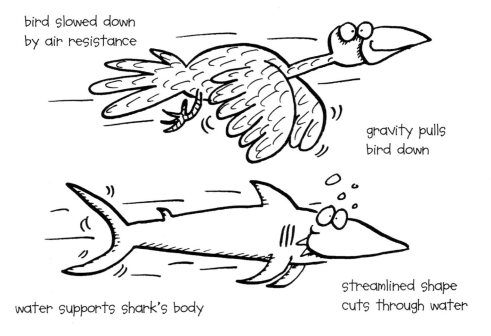

bird slowed down by air resistance

gravity pulls bird down

water supports shark's body

streamlined shape cuts through water

The shark's streamlined shape reduces the amount of friction caused by the water and enables the shark to move quickly through the water.

Well got all that? Now you can relax – it's the moment you've been waiting for... it's story time!

15

Boy on a bike

Charlotte was trying out her new bike when she saw the mysterious boy who was to save her life. It was a bright April afternoon and she was pedalling up the long hill from Southam Road, enjoying the wind on her face and the quiet whirr of the wheels.

The bike was MEGA-FANTABULOUS (Charlotte liked making up words) and she gazed fondly at its gleaming green paintwork and bright silver chrome. The wheel spokes were a glimmering blur and the tarmac flowed under its tyres like a dark river. As the slope rose the bike slowed and Charlotte clicked into a lower gear. Just then she saw the boy.

IT'S A FACT
Moving bicycles are stable because the movement of the turning wheels keeps them from falling.

IT'S A FACT
Using the correct gear allows you to go up slopes without having to push the pedals down so hard.

He was riding his bike directly across the road from her. A thin boy with very short hair and old-fashioned grey shorts on an old black bike that appeared too large for him. The boy glanced at Charlotte, and his dark eyes seemed to challenge her.

She looked away embarrassed and pedalled harder against the rising slope. So he wanted a race – well, Charlotte would show him! The boy was ahead now, pedalling effortlessly as Charlotte puffed and panted. She gritted her teeth.

IT'S A FACT
Cycling up a slope against the wind means that you must push against the wind and also against the force of your own weight being pulled down the hill by gravity.

'This is TERRIBUBBLE!' she thought crossly. 'GRRR – no boy beats Charlotte Heathfield!' Then a bus shot past, hiding the boy from view, and when Charlotte looked again he was gone. Perhaps he'd turned into the road opposite, but there was no sign of him now. Charlotte was frowning as she pedalled home.

The next day was bright and sunny and Charlotte was looking forward to another ride – but the bike's front wheel was flat. It had punctured! Charlotte screwed up her face in annoyance. She felt like screaming – but that would only wake Dad who had just gone to bed after his nightshift.

'OH HORRAGROAN!' she exclaimed, sticking out her

tongue at the cat. Then with a sinking feeling in her heart she set out on a very delicate mission.

Stephen was in his room. He was always in his room, but it was after eleven, so he was probably awake.

'Be in a good mood,' Charlotte prayed. She knocked on his door.

'What?' said a muffled voice.

'Brother dearest - how would you like a nice cold drink?'

'What do you want?'

'I've got a punctilio.'

Charlotte risked opening the door. There was a whiff of sweat and dirty clothes from the room. Stephen was sitting propped up on his bed reading a science book. As usual there was stubble on his bony chin and his hair looked unwashed. (But then, Stephen was in his second year of a physics course!) Charlotte caught a glimpse of what looked like radio parts on the floor.

'Talk properly!' he said gruffly.

'Please, please – dearest, darling brotherburble.'

'Later.'

18

It was almost lunchtime when Stephen set to work.

'I have to apply a force to stretch the rubber tyre over the rim,' he explained. 'Then the tyre levers can remove the tyre because of the lever action – see.'

Charlotte pretended to stifle a yawn. The corners of Stephen's mouth turned down grumpily.

'Well, don't ask me to do your science homework!'

'I won't – so there!' said Charlotte.

'Yeah, well this is interesting. The rubber of the tyres provides friction to grip the road and the air-filled inner tube soaks up any bumps and gives you a smooth ride.'

Stephen pulled out the limp inner tube and began searching for the puncture hole.

It was a few days later and Charlotte's dad was driving her gran to the hospital.

'Never liked those places,' said gran for the third time.

'You'll be alright gran,' said Charlotte, leaning forward from the back and squeezing her pale, listless hand. Charlotte's gran smiled weakly. She had wavy white hair and watery blue eyes.

'If you've got your health you don't have to worry,' she said. 'That's what your grandpa used to say, rest his soul. Mind you, I haven't got my health now. He was like you, Charlotte. He would have been so proud of your running trophies.'

'Are you belted up Charlotte?' asked her dad who was driving.

'Yeah, belt up,' said Stephen, waking from a scientific day dream. 'If this car crashed you'd be thrown forward. BAM! Straight through the windscreen.'

'You're a GROSSA-SLUMPO, Stephen!'

> **IT'S A FACT**
> When a car brakes the people continue to move forward unless stopped by another force. Seat belts provide this force and keep you in your seat.

'Mind that cyclist!' cried Charlotte's mum, who was in the back with the children.

'I can see her!' snapped Charlotte's dad.

'He was a cyclist too,' mused Charlotte's gran. 'Your grandpa, I mean. He was always talking about his bike when I first met him.'

'I didn't know bikes had been invented then!' said Stephen.

'Blooming cheek – I bet he'd have been keen on this cycle race. You are going in for it aren't you, Charlotte?'

'What race?' said Charlotte curiously.

'The Family Fun Day Race. They're going all around

the neighbourhood and there's a prize for the winner.'

'Um...' said Charlotte uncertainly.

'Oh, give it a go!' Charlotte's gran pleaded. 'You're bound to win!'

'Yeah,' said Stephen 'and I could be your mechanic – that's if you give me a share of your winnings!'

A week later Charlotte was having a bad day. How could her Mum accuse her of not feeding the cat when it was Stephen's turn and he never did it! Then her mum had said that gran wasn't getting any better. Now Charlotte felt like crying – in fact she felt MEGA-GROANABUBBLE! And that's why she was cycling on the road when her mum told her she should always go on the pavement. The cars roared down behind her,

IT'S A FACT
When Charlotte is pedalling she overcomes the resistance of friction from the ground and moving parts of her bike. If she stops pedalling, this friction would slow and then stop her bike (see page 11).

their engines seeming to rise and then fall as they passed her. It had been raining and the road was black and slick beneath her wheels.

She was heading down the slope towards Southam Road faster

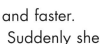

and faster. Suddenly she saw the boy. This time he was on the pavement holding his bike. Watching her with his strange dark eyes, waiting for her.

Charlotte braked hard. The bike wouldn't stop! She stuck her trainers out and dragged the bike to a halt, jerking forward in her seat.

IT'S A FACT
The brake blocks are forced against the rim of the wheel and friction between the block and wheel slows the bike.

Just then there was a heavy rattle and roar as a huge lorry thundered past. It was exactly where Charlotte would have been if she hadn't braked early! Charlotte looked around but the boy had gone. Her legs felt like jelly as she dragged her bicycle on to the pavement.

Every day after school, Charlotte practised for the race, but she never cycled on the road again and she never saw the boy. The day of the race roared towards her like an express train. All too soon the big moment arrived.

Charlotte fiddled nervously with the strap of her safely helmet. Then, realizing that the race was about to begin, she stood with her right foot on the pedal of her bicycle and her left foot on the road. The machine leaned under her. A line of children stood in similar positions looking expectantly at a man with a starting pistol. And just then Charlotte saw the boy. She gasped in shock.

He was at the end of the line, his head down and his pale hands clutching the handlebars of his old black bicycle. No one seemed to have noticed him except Charlotte's gran, who was staring at the boy in a daze.

Then the pistol fired.

IT'S A FACT

By crouching Charlotte reduced the area of her body facing the wind and so reduced drag. She used the force of her weight to change the direction of the bike.

Everything happened very fast. Later, Charlotte would remember her feet pushing hard on the pedals and the bike swaying under her. She crouched against the wind as she shot past the long lines of people.

Their cheers and shouts sounded distant. And all the

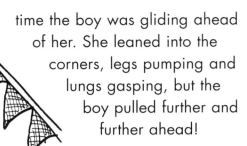

time the boy was gliding ahead of her. She leaned into the corners, legs pumping and lungs gasping, but the boy pulled further and further ahead!

Someone shouted encouragement. Then she saw the finishing line. Flags were stretched across the lane at the back of Calcross Street. There was even a man with a chequered flag. But Charlotte knew that she wouldn't win. The boy would get there first, his thin legs pedalling madly.

'Sorry gran,' she said to herself, 'I did my best.'
She made one last effort and shot across the line. SECOND!

Then she saw her dad waving and yelling 'STOP!'
She braked.
It was like a film. Charlotte and her bike went over – gravel flying in a big cloud of dust. She felt her knee bash the ground. Then she was sprawling – there was dirt on her shorts and blood on her leg.

> **IT'S A FACT**
> As the wheels lock the bike still moves forwards. Tiny differences between the braking force on each wheel will skid the bike around.

People were shouting, others were running towards her.
The boy had gone.
Charlotte's knee was hurting now.

'Are you hurt?' Charlotte's mum cried, helping her up and hugging her.

'The boy... where is he?' she asked her mum.

'What boy?'

'Yes, what boy?' said Charlotte's dad, sounding puzzled.

'Hey Charlotte, you look like you've seen a ghost,' said Stephen.

Then a voice rang out from the tannoy:
'AND THE WINNER IS CHARLOTTE HEATHFIELD!'

Charlotte couldn't believe her ears, her knee was really hurting now. 'I saw a boy!' she said fiercely, her eyes filling with tears. 'I saw him, why won't anyone believe me?'

Then Charlotte's gran came and held her tight.
'I saw him too,' she said quietly. 'That boy was your grandpa as I knew him 69 years ago. He must have come back to watch over you.'

QUIZ TIME

Here's your chance to test your brain against some quickie, quirky, quality quizzes. Will you be left puzzling?

WHAT HAPPENED NEXT?

In this quiz all you have to do is say what happens next...

1 Astronaut Alan Shepard drops a hammer and a feather on the moon. What happens next?

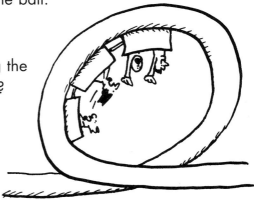

a The hammer and the feather hit the ground at the same time.

b The hammer falls faster than the feather.

2 Two astronauts are playing a ball game in space... What happens to the astronaut when he throws the ball?

a He moves forwards after the ball.

b He moves backwards.

3 These children are looping the loop. What happens to them?

a They're pinned to their seats.

b They fall to the ground.

FRICTION QUIZ

Friction makes some of these objects harder to shift than others.
Can you place them in order of ease of movement?
Start with the easiest...

a Sliding a lump of ice across a skating rink.

b Pushing a wooden crate over a brick patio.

c Flexing your arm at the elbow.

d Pushing a wooden crate across a polished wooden floor.

MATCH THEM UP

In this quiz you're given the questions and the answers – you just need to match them up! It's simple-dimple!

1 What happens to a golf ball after it's whacked?

2 What happens to the sole of your trainer when it hits the pavement?

3 What happens to a pole vaulter's pole?

Answers

a It bends and then straightens.

b It gets squashed out of shape.

c Shock waves pass across its surface.

The answers are on the following page.

QUIZ TIME ANSWERS

WHAT HAPPENED NEXT

1a As long as there isn't any air to cause drag, all falling objects fall at the same rate. Of course, there isn't any air on the moon.

2b Remember Newton's third law? If you throw a ball, the ball pushes back with an equal force. On Earth you don't often notice this, but in space the force from the ball would cause you to move backwards.

3a The rollercoaster applies a force to the passengers to make them change direction as they go round in a circle. This is the force that pins them to their seats. The safety bar is only needed if the rollercoaster breaks down!

FRICTION

easy!

c The major joints of the body are surrounded by fluid which allows them to move with scarcely any friction. If you didn't have this you might squeak as you walk.

a Ice on ice is very slippery. A thin layer of ice melts and ensures that there is very little friction.

d The wooden floor is smoother than the bricks and so there is less friction.

b There's lots of friction between the rough bricks and the rough wooden crate.

MATCH THEM UP

1b The golf club passes on the full force of its swing to the ball, and the force hits only a small area. This impact squashes the ball out of shape, but it immediately bounces back and zooms off.

2c Tiny shock waves are caused by friction between the rubber and the ground.

3a The pole has elasticity (see page 9). It bends as it soaks up the energy of the impact with the ground and releases the energy as it straightens. This helps to catapult the vaulter over the bar.

29

SCIENCE SUPERSTARS

Meet some of the people who uncovered the mysteries of forces – you might call them the 'movers and shakers' of the science world!

To begin at the beginning...
Early people had no idea why forces worked, but by trial and error they invented the bow and arrow (about 40,000 BC) and the wheel (3500 BC), both of which use forces in an efficient way. But the first explanations proved to be a false dawn...

ARISTOTLE
384–322 BC
Nationality: Greek
Claim to fame: influenced science
for over 1800 years.

Aristotle spent most of his life as a teacher in Athens, although he travelled in Turkey and tutored the future king, Alexander the Great. His teaching covered everything, but although his work on biology

was based on observation (he cut up dead animals), his ideas on forces were based on reasoning. Faulty reasoning. He thought that the stars and planets were set in see-through spheres that revolved around the Earth, and he claimed that heavy objects fell faster than light objects. Aristotle's ideas were taken as the final word by scholars for 1800 years.

BELIEVE IT OR NOT!

Aristotle's works were lost, but in 80 BC some of them were found in a pit by a Roman soldier. The action of this unknown man shaped the history of science for 1700 years!

GALILEO GALILEI

1564–1642
Nationality: Italian
Claim to fame: overturned
Aristotle's ideas on forces.

Galileo was brilliant at everything he attempted – he even discovered the principle of the pendulum by timing a swinging lamp during a church sermon.

Unlike Aristotle, Galileo used observation and experiments to find out scientific truths. By rolling balls down slopes he proved that objects pick up speed at the same rate regardless of weight. Then Galileo challenged Aristotle's ideas about astronomy by showing that Venus went round the Sun rather than the

Earth. This brought Galileo into conflict with the Church, which had accepted Aristotle's ideas as Christian beliefs. In 1633 Galileo was put on trial and forced to admit he was wrong (even though he was right).

BELIEVE IT OR NOT!

Galileo's dad wanted him to study medicine but Galileo wanted to study maths — so he studied maths in secret until his dad changed his mind.

ISAAC NEWTON

1642–1727
Nationality: British
Claim to fame: explained forces in mathematical terms.

Isaac Newton was a dreamy boy who spent his time building toy machines and thinking scientific thoughts. At university Isaac was very poor and had to work as a servant. He spent his money on scientific equipment, such as a prism to split light into colours. During a spell at home he began thinking about gravity (perhaps after seeing an apple fall from a tree), and in 1685 his work led to the

Principia, the greatest scientific book ever, containing Newton's theory of gravity and his laws of motion. Despite his fame, Newton was a gloomy humourless man who is said to have laughed only once in his entire life.

BELIEVE IT OR NOT!

The *Principia* was published because of a murder. Newton wasn't rich enough to pay the printer so the work was funded by Newton's friend, Edmond Halley (1656–1742). Halley only had the cash because he had inherited a fortune after his dad had been mysteriously killed.

AND TODAY...

Newton's laws are still used for designing everything from skyscrapers to seatbelts, but the work of Albert Einstein (1879–1955) on gravity is now used by astronomers to study mysterious objects, such as black holes.

Coming up next – your chance to try your hand at being a Galileo or Newton with a few experiments!

SECRET SCIENCE EXPERIMENTS

We've taken a peek at the notes of physicist Frieda Throw. Her experiments are guaranteed free from explosions or stinks, but they're still fun (honest!)

Dear Reader

I've allowed you to look at my notebooks on one condition. You must perform your experiments like a proper scientist. This means that if you do an experiment make sure you record your results and if you're not sure what they were, repeat the experiment again to check. If you do this, make sure you use the same equipment in the same way to ensure that it's a fair test. HAVE FUN, MY DEARS!

Frieda Throw

TEST YOUR MUSCLES

Anyone can do this experiment – even people with weedy little muscles like my husband Mr Throw. So don't be afraid to chance your arm!

❶ Flex your arm as strongly as you can so that your forearm is on top of your upper arm.

❷ Without relaxing your upper arm muscles, try to push your forearm back and so straighten your arm with your other arm.

34

Here's what happens ...
You won't be able to! Why not?

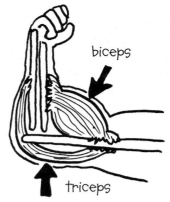

biceps

triceps

The biceps muscle flexes the arm, and the triceps muscle straightens it.

SCIENCE SECRET
Your arm movements are controlled by two muscles. Both muscles are anchored to your arm bones and make them move, but the biceps is bigger and stronger and that's why you can't straighten your arm.

WEIRD WEIGHT LOSS
Well, my dears, when I discovered this experiment I almost danced on the bathroom scales! Not that I've got a weight problem, you understand, it's the science that makes it so exciting!

YOU WILL NEED
★ A pair of bathroom scales
★ A human body (why not use your own?)

❶ Stand on the scales and note your weight.

❷ Keep your eye on the weight indicator and lift your arms.

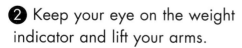

❸ What happens to the weight indicator when you lower your arms? Try it.

Here's what happens...

The weight indicator will swing wildly, but your weight appears to increase briefly as your lift your arms and decrease as you lower your arms. Why is this?

SCIENCE SECRET

As you lift your arms an equal force tries to push them down. It succeeds in pushing your body down on the scales and briefly increases your weight. When you lower your arms the opposite force pushes upwards and appears to lighten you.

I CAN'T STAND IT!

All you need is a friend and if you've got no one handy you could experiment on yourself. I tried it on Mr Throw – he certainly couldn't stand this experiment!

YOU WILL NEED
★ A friend
★ An ordinary upright chair
★ A finger (make sure it's attached to your hand)

1 Sit your friend on the chair.

2 Press your forefinger firmly against her forehead.

3 Ask her to stand up. Will she be able to?

Here's what happens...
They can't! Can you explain why not?

SCIENCE SECRET
In order to stand up, your friend must shift her centre of gravity
(that's the expression we scientists use to describe the point
around which the gravitational force is exactly balanced).
Anyway, she must shift her centre of gravity from her bottom
to her feet and she can only do this by moving her head
forward. Your finger stops her head moving and so she
can't stand up. She's pinned down by gravity!

SPEEDY SERVICE
Don't copy me, my dears, and use the best tea service.
It took me ages to pick up the pieces and Mr Throw wasn't
too happy either!

YOU WILL NEED
★ A plastic, I repeat P-L-A-S-T-I-C glass.
★ A tea towel

1 Place the tea towel
on a work surface with
the end of the tea
towel hanging off the
edge of the surface.

2 Half fill the glass with water and place it on the tea towel.

3 Cross your fingers (this precaution isn't scientifically necessary).

4 Whip the tea towel from under the glass. (You will need to pull the cloth down as well as away from the glass.)

Here's what happens...
The glass remains on the table... hopefully. Can you achieve this trick without spilling any water? Why is this possible?

SCIENCE SECRET
Skilled performers can pull away a tablecloth from underneath an entire dinner service (don't even think of trying this!)
The reason why it's possible is that the inertia of the glass is greater than the friction from the moving cloth – so the glass stays where it is.

NEED A LIFT?

Feeling a bit crushed, my dears? It's the weight of all that air pressing down on you! Every moment of the day you are being crushed by air which weighs the same as two elephants, but the air inside your body is pushing back equally hard. Anyway, this experiment shows what air pressure can do...

YOU WILL NEED
★ A table
★ A ruler
★ Two pages of a newspaper (if the newspaper is a big one a single page will do)

1 Place the newspaper on the table next to the edge.

2 Place the ruler under the newspaper so that one end sticks out over the edge of the table by 5 cm.

3 Bring your fist down on the exposed part of the ruler. What do you think happens next?

Here's what happens...
You were expecting the newspaper to go flying weren't you? Well, it doesn't! Why ever not?

SCIENCE SECRET
The newspaper is being pinned to the table by the air pushing down on it – a weight of two tonnes! This force is called air pressure, and it's stronger than the force of the ruler rising up.

Pillars of Power

They say the pen is mightier than the sword my dears, but it isn't as mighty as a piece of paper!

YOU WILL NEED
★ An A4 piece of paper
★ An elastic band
★ Paperback books
★ Kitchen scales
★ A ruler

The practical bit...

1 Roll the paper into a roll 6 cm across.

2 Stretch an elastic band around the centre of the roll.

3 Set the roll on end. Weigh a book, note the weight and lay the bookon top of the rolled-up paper.

Here's what happens...

The piece of paper isn't squashed flat even though it weighs far less than the book!

SCIENCE SECRET

1 The forces acting on the rolled-up paper are balanced and the elastic band holds the sides and stops them from buckling.

2 Pillars are great for holding up objects. Your paper pillar should support up to 800 grams of books and real pillars can hold up huge buildings.

THE LAST STRAW

I thought this trick was ever so funny when I tried it on my husband at a party. Mr Throw didn't see the joke!

YOU WILL NEED
★ A drinking straw
★ A drink
★ A pin
★ A ruler

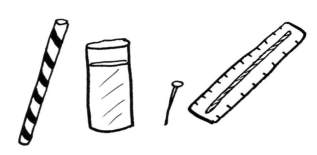

The practical bit...

1 Use the pin to make two holes in the straw. One hole should be 2 cm from one end of the straw and the other hole should be 2 cm from the opposite end of the straw.

2 Try to suck the drink through the straw.

Here's what happens...
It's very, very hard!

SCIENCE SECRET

1 A straw works because air pressure in your mouth as it sucks is less than the air pressure pushing down on the drink from above. This difference in pressure pushes the drink up the straw as you suck.

2 Air pushes through the holes in the straw, increasing the air pressure and this makes it really hard to suck up the drink.

★ GOBSMACKING GRAVITY

A scientist used his measurement of gravity to weigh the Earth. In 1798 eccentric boffin Henry Cavendish (1731–1810) filled a room with two large lead balls and two small ones all hanging from the ceiling. He measured the gravitational pull of the larger balls on the smaller, and used this to calculate the weight of the Earth to 6000 billion billion tonnes. He was just 24 billion billion tonnes out (hmm – details, details).

★ LOSING WEIGHT

The further you go away from the ground the weaker the force of gravity becomes. This means that when you go for a flight in a plane you actually lose weight slightly!

★ BLACK HOLES

Black holes have a massive gravitational pull because their huge mass is crammed into a small area. Their gravity is so strong that even light can't escape – that's why they're black. To make the Earth into a black hole you would have to squeeze the entire planet until it's just 18 mm across – breathe in now!

★ EINSTEIN'S CUPPA

In 1926 famous scientist Albert Einstein explained why tea leaves settle in the centre of the bottom of a tea cup after you stir the tea. The great man pondered the problem for a while. Then he explained that the tea leaves were pushed into the centre by forces at the top of the liquid caused by the shape of the tea cup, and by friction around the edges of the cup. Obviously science really was Einstein's cup of tea.

★ WHISTLING ROCKETS

In the First World War rockets carried messages. The gunpowder-filled rockets carried the message in a nose cone together with a whistle. When air rushed through a hole, the whistle blew, warning people to get out of the way. A rim around the nose, called a flange, increased the force of drag and controlled how far the rocket went.

★ NO FLYING CARS

Did you know that racing cars have upside-down wings? Aircraft wings lift the plane up in the air. But the upside-down wings of a racing car have the opposite effect. They produce more friction, pinning the car to the track and stopping it from taking off at speed!

★ BUNGEE JUMPING

The sport of bungee jumping isn't modern. The native people of Pentecost Island, Vanuatu, have a traditional festival in which they jump off high towers with lianas (creepers) tied around their ankles. Like a bungee rope, the elastic creeper breaks the fall just as the person is about to hit the ground.

★ EGGSCELLENT!

Eggshells are thin, but eggs themselves are surprisingly strong. Well, they don't crack if a bird sits on them (OK they might crack if you sat on them). The curved eggshell ensures that the force is spread around its edges rather than being concentrated at one point. A cycle helmet works in the same way but of course it's much stronger. Eggscellent idea – eh?

★ TWIST AND SHAKE!

Skyscrapers are designed to sway in the wind – but in 1986 the Hong Kong and Shanghai Bank building in Hong Kong was found to be twisting too. All the windows had to be secured with special springy glue so that they wouldn't be twisted out of their frames. This must have driven the architects round the twist.

44

OOPS!

Although computer simulations are used to prepare a new building for every force that might affect it, things do go wrong. In 1978 the roof of the huge Long Island University auditorium fell in. The wind had blown a fall of snow over to one side and created an unbalanced force.

whoops!

IT'S TOO LATE

Have you ever wondered why one kilogram weighs one kilogram? The weight was invented in 1791 as the weight of a litre of water at 4°C. A special block of metal was forged that weighed exactly one kilogram and it was displayed in Paris. Unfortunately, later measurements showed that the litre of water weighed slightly less than one kilogram. But by then it was too late to change the measurement.

Goodbye...

Sadly we've run out of space! Never mind, if you've read this far you'll know that forces are not only fundamental to how the universe works – they're intriguing too. OOPS – I nearly forgot that fly on the windscreen! When a fly splats on to a windscreen, the glass actually dents with the force of the impact and then bounces back producing a vibration which makes the SPLAT sound? Fascinating – eh?

you bet!

GLOSSARY

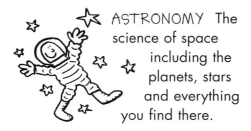

ASTRONOMY The science of space including the planets, stars and everything you find there.

ATOMS The tiny units that make up all materials.

BICEPS/TRICEPS Muscles in the upper arm. The biceps flexes the arm and the triceps straightens it.

BLACK HOLE A space object with a huge mass for its size. Black holes have powerful gravity and suck in anything that comes near.

DRAG This is the force that slows an object as it moves through air or a liquid such as water.

ELASTICITY The amount an object can be squashed or stretched without breaking.

FRICTION The force created when two objects rub together. Friction can be reduced by putting a slippery substance like oil between the two surfaces.

HALLEY, EDMOND (1656–1742) An astronomer who mapped many of the stars of the southern sky. Halley's comet is named after him.

INERTIA When objects either stay where they are when they are not moving or carry on moving until affected by another force.

LAW In science a law is an important fact that can be checked by observation and experiment and holds true for different conditions.

46

LEVER A bar that swings on a pivot called a fulcrum. A lever helps to lift or move a load. By moving one end of the lever a long way you can move the other end a short distance, but with greater force.

MASS The amount of material an object contains. A cannon ball has a greater mass than a beach ball and that's why it feels heavier even though it's smaller.

METEORITE A lump of rock or metal that falls from outer space and hits the earth.

PENDULUM A swinging weight on the end of a rod or string.

POLE The name for one end of a magnet. Each magnet has two ends – a north pole and a south pole.

PRISM A see-through triangular shape.

ROSIN A sticky substance made from pine wood. Rosin is used as an ingredient in some soaps and paints.

SPRING BALANCE A simple weighing machine on which weight or force can be measured by pulling on a spring.

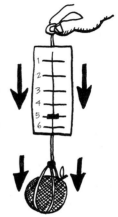

STREAMLINED A sleek, smooth shape designed to reduce the effects of drag.

UPTHRUST The force that pushes upwards on an object in a liquid such as water.

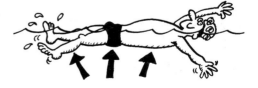

WEIGHT The force of gravity on an object. Weight depends partly on the mass of the object (see above) and partly on the strength of the force of gravity.

INDEX